Nature's Wonders

SARA LOUISE KRAS

 **Marshall Cavendish**
Benchmark
New York

Marshall Cavendish Benchmark
99 White Plains Road
Tarrytown, NY 10591
www.marshallcavendish.us

Expert Reader: Dr. Leonard Berry, Director, Florida Center for Environmental Studies,
Palm Beach Gardens, Florida

All Internet addresses were correct and accurate at the time of printing.

Library of Congress Cataloging-in-Publication Data
Kras, Sara Louise.
The Everglades / by Sara Louise Kras.
p. cm. — (Nature's wonders)
Summary: "Provides comprehensive information on the geography, history, wildlife, peoples, and environmental
issues of the Everglades"—Provided by publisher.
Includes bibliographical references and index.
ISBN 978-0-7614-3931-8
1. Everglades National Park (Fla.)—Juvenile literature. I. Title.
F317.E9K73 2010
975.9'39—dc22
2008011694

Editor: Christine Florie
Publisher: Michelle Bisson
Art Director: Anahid Hamparian
Series Designer: Kay Petronio

Photo research by Connie Gardner

Cover photo by Peter Bisset/Getty Images

The photographs in this book are used by permission and through the courtesy of: *North Wind Picture Archives:* 1,
52–53; *Corbis:* Galen Rowell, 3, 76; Tim Wright, 14; Franz Marc Frei, 22–23, 24; Steve Kaufman, 40; David Muench,
44; Morton Beebe, 62; Kevin Flemming, 71; Wayne Bennett, 83; *AP Photo:* Pat Carter, 64, 81; Kathy Willens, 68; *Super
Stock:* Donna and Steve O'Meara, 4; James Urbach, 34; Barry Mansell, 35; *Joe Kras Photography:* 7, 17, 18, 28, 38, 88;
Getty Images: Mary Liz Austin, 13; David Tipling, 26; MPI, 56; Peter Essick, 60–61; Willard R. Culver, 66; Robert
Nickelsberg, 78; *The Granger Collection:* 48, 51, 55, 59; *Bridgeman Art Library:* Collecting Crops for the Communal
Storehouse, From "Brevis Narration", engraved by Theodore de Bry (1528–88) published in Frankfurt, 1591
(coloured engraving), 50; *Minden Pictures:* Tom Verzo, 31; Rolf Nussbaumer, 42; Norbert Wu, 43; Fred Bavendam,
85; Tui De Roy, 90; *Dembinsky Photo Associates:* Bill Lea, 10–11, Barbara Gerlach, 32; John Gerlach, 37; *Art Life Images:*
age footstock, back cover, 20, 36; *Alamy:* David Newham, 47 (B); *Gibson Stock Photography:* 19; *The Image Works:* Jeff
Greenberg, 72; *Animals/Animals:* Zigmund Leszczynski, 41; *Photo Researchers:* Anne Hubbard, 45; *Digital Railroad:*
John Decker, 47 (T).

Maps (p.6 and p.15) by Mapping Specialists Limited

Printed in Malaysia

1 3 5 6 4 2

ONE

A Place of Quiet Beauty

On the open sawgrass plains of southern Florida are wetlands called the Everglades. Alligators silently move through shallow water, which flows between huge cypress trees with branches that are decorated with air plants. Flocks of colorful wading birds pick their way among thick, green ferns as they search for fish.

Flitting through the moist, sweet-smelling air of the Everglades are colorful butterflies and large, hovering dragonflies. In a landscape without hills, the sky seems endless.

The Everglades wetlands consist of vast sawgrass prairies, immense freshwater bays and lakes, mangrove forests, and the Florida Bay. Bordered by the Gulf of Mexico and the Atlantic Ocean, the bay is located at the southern tip of Florida. The slow-moving river making up the Everglades wetlands is 50 miles (80 kilometers) wide in some areas and flows only about a quarter of a mile (0.4 km) a day. Its depth ranges from 6 inches (15 centimeters) to about 1 foot (0.3 meter).

◀ *The Everglades in South Florida is the largest subtropical wetland in the United States.*

GEOPOLITICAL MAP OF THE EVERGLADES

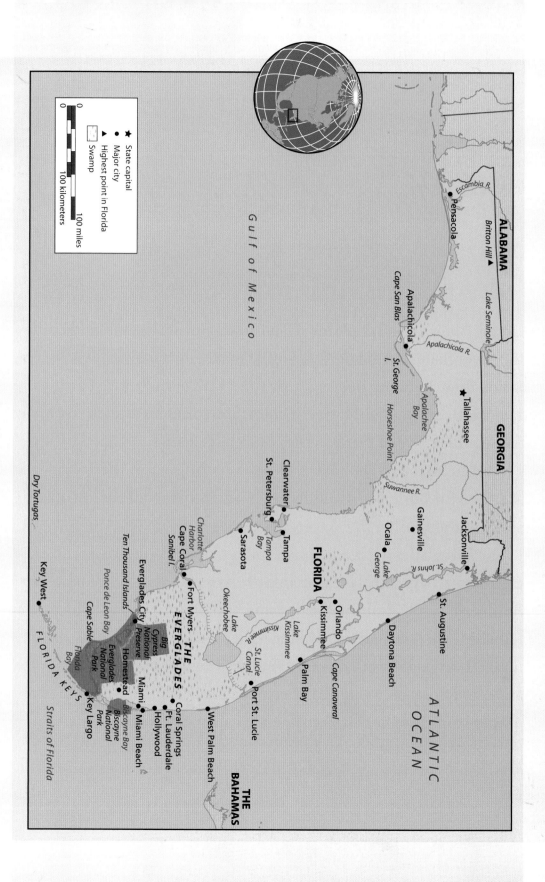

State capital
Major city
Highest point in Florida
Swamp

0 100 kilometers
0 100 miles

ALABAMA

GEORGIA

FLORIDA

THE BAHAMAS

Gulf of Mexico

ATLANTIC OCEAN

Britton Hill ▲
Lake Seminole
Escambia R.
Pensacola

Apalachicola
Cape San Blas
St. George I.
Apalachicola R.
Apalachee Bay
Horseshoe Point
Suwannee R.

★ Tallahassee

Gainesville
Ocala
Lake George
St. Johns R.
Jacksonville

St. Augustine

Daytona Beach

Orlando
Kissimmee
Lake Kissimmee
Kissimmee R.
Cape Canaveral

Palm Bay

Port St. Lucie
St. Lucie Canal

West Palm Beach

Lake Okeechobee

Clearwater
St. Petersburg
Tampa Bay
Tampa
Sarasota

Charlotte Harbor
Cape Coral
Sanibel I.

Fort Myers

Ten Thousand Islands
Everglades City

THE EVERGLADES

Big Cypress National Preserve

Homestead
Everglades National Park

Coral Springs
Ft. Lauderdale
Hollywood
Miami
Miami Beach
Biscayne Bay
Biscayne National Park

Ponce de Leon Bay
Cape Sable
Florida Bay

Key Largo

Dry Tortugas

Key West

FLORIDA KEYS

Straits of Florida

Less than one hundred years ago, the Everglades was a large shallow river, moving slowly from Lake Okeechobee in central Florida to the mangrove forests of Florida Bay. In more recent years, the activities of people have reshaped the Everglades to what remains today.

SOUNDS AND SIGHTS

The Everglades can be a place of immense quiet. Occasionally there are cackles and croaks from large wading birds or pig frogs. A splash of water could mean that an alligator is sliding off the riverbank or an anhinga is catching a fish. A great blue heron wades silently on thin legs, sometimes shaking its head to get rid of pesky gnats.

The famous Everglades **environmentalist**, Marjory Stoneman Douglas, once said while visiting the Everglades, "I love it here. The minute I get here I seem to breathe deep." She went on to say, "I always thought the Everglades would teach the American people how to be quiet."

An egret silently wades through sawgrass.

Establishing Everglades National Park

Once people began to settle the area of the original Everglades, the "river of grass," so named by Marjory Stoneman Douglas, it began diminishing rapidly. Even before that, during the early 1900s, many of the beautiful birds of the Everglades were hunted to almost extinction. To save them, a portion of the Everglades was set aside in 1916 to protect the animals from hunters. This area was called the Royal Palm State Park. Years later, on December 6, 1947, President Harry S. Truman dedicated Everglades National Park, the country's first park to be set aside because of its unique ecosystems. Among the thousands who attended the dedication were Marjory Stoneman Douglas and Ernest F. Coe, another well-known Everglades environmentalist. It is important to remember that Everglades National Park is a very small section of the original Everglades.

WORLDWIDE IMPORTANCE

At a little over 1.5 million acres (610,684 hectares), the Everglades is the third-largest park on the mainland United States. It is also the largest wilderness area east of the Rocky Mountains. In North America, the Everglades has the biggest continuous section of sawgrass prairie and is the most important breeding area for tropical wading birds.

In 1976, in recognition of its worldwide importance, the Everglades was designated an International Biosphere Reserve by the United Nations Educational, Scientific and Cultural Organization (UNESCO). An International Biosphere Reserve is a protected area consisting of land and water, representing a balanced relationship between humans and nature. In 1979 Everglades National Park became a World Heritage Site. UNESCO assigned this label because of the area's unique combination of human history and wide variety of plants and animals, including threatened and endangered species.

On June 4, 1987, Everglades National Park was named a Wetland of International Importance by the Convention on Wetlands in Ramsar, Iran. This term applies to natural areas that not only contain endangered species and a wide variety of animals and plants, but also support animals during their development.

THE FUTURE OF THE EVERGLADES

The Everglades is an endangered natural site that is close to becoming extinct. Its entire **ecosystem,** including its trees, grass, insects, and other living things, is starting to fail because there is not enough freshwater to sustain it.

Watched by the entire world, the U.S. government and the state of Florida are trying to save the Everglades. If they are successful, it will be the largest natural restoration of its kind. If the plan works, the techniques used will be implemented in other endangered areas around the world.

◄ *The Everglades has one of the most diverse ecosystems in the world. This grants it worldwide importance.*

TWO

A Landscape Formed by Water

The various landscapes of the Everglades have one thing in common: they were shaped by water. Over the last five thousand years, the Glades ecosystems have been acquiring the forms we see today. It all began when a sea covered much of what is present-day Florida. Over time, the shells of dead aquatic creatures formed into a rock called limestone. When the sea receded, the Florida peninsula appeared. Beneath the southern part of the peninsula, honeycombed limestone **aquifers** filled with rainwater.

The aquifers were created when water traveled downward from the surface of the earth into the limestone layer. Holes formed in the limestone, and water accumulated there. Today, most of the drinking water used by residents of southern Florida comes from aquifers.

◀ *The Everglades is a slow-moving river that features tropical plants, swamps, pinelands, and hammocks.*

THE ORIGINAL EVERGLADES

The original Everglades was very different from what we see today. The yearly cycle of the Everglades began in bodies of water known as the Kissimmee chain of lakes. In the past, the Kissimmee lakes flowed into the Kissimmee River **basin**. In the broad basin, the water created large wetlands where thousands of wading birds gathered. It took the waters of the Kissimmee River eleven days to flow south to Lake Okeechobee.

Lake Okeechobee is not deep, and when it overflowed, a river was created. Its waters continue south toward Florida Bay. A variety of plants and animals became dependent on this slow-moving river, later called the Everglades.

◄ *The winding waters of the Everglades pass through mangrove forests and swamplands.*

MAP OF THE EVERGLADES

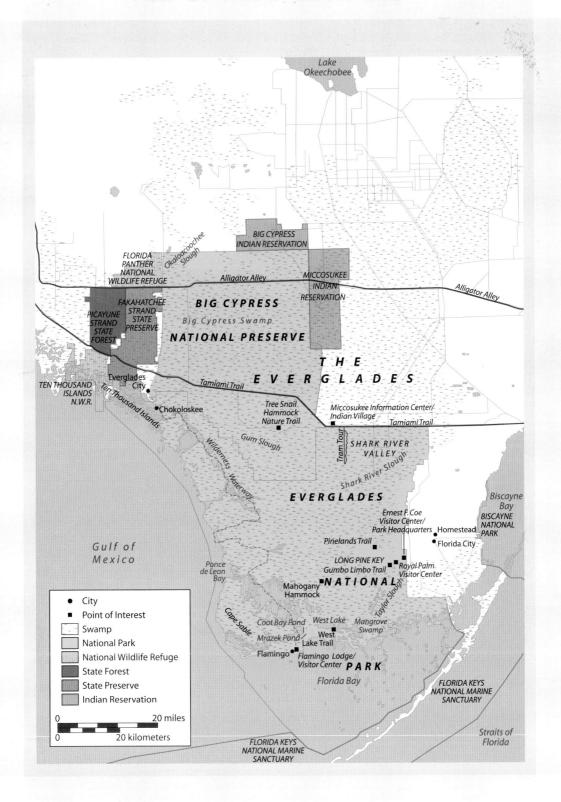

Lake Okeechobee

BIG CYPRESS INDIAN RESERVATION

FLORIDA PANTHER NATIONAL WILDLIFE REFUGE

Okaloacoochee Slough

Alligator Alley

MICCOSUKEE INDIAN RESERVATION

Alligator Alley

FAKAHATCHEE STRAND STATE PRESERVE

PICAYUNE STRAND STATE FOREST

BIG CYPRESS

Big Cypress Swamp

NATIONAL PRESERVE

THE EVERGLADES

TEN THOUSAND ISLANDS N.W.R.

Everglades City

Ten Thousand Islands

Tamiami Trail

Chokoloskee

Tree Snail Hammock Nature Trail

Miccosukee Information Center/ Indian Village

Tamiami Trail

Gum Slough

Tram Tour

SHARK RIVER VALLEY

Wilderness Waterway

Shark River Slough

EVERGLADES

Biscayne Bay

BISCAYNE NATIONAL PARK

Ernest F. Coe Visitor Center/ Park Headquarters

Homestead

Florida City

Pinelands Trail

Gulf of Mexico

Ponce de Leon Bay

LONG PINE KEY Gumbo Limbo Trail

Royal Palm Visitor Center

Mahogany Hammock

NATIONAL

Taylor Slough

Cape Sable

Coot Bay Pond

West Lake

Mangrove Swamp

Mrazek Pond

West Lake Trail

Flamingo

Flamingo Lodge/ Visitor Center

PARK

Florida Bay

FLORIDA KEYS NATIONAL MARINE SANCTUARY

Straits of Florida

FLORIDA KEYS NATIONAL MARINE SANCTUARY

Legend

- • City
- ■ Point of Interest
- Swamp
- National Park
- National Wildlife Refuge
- State Forest
- State Preserve
- Indian Reservation

0 — 20 miles
0 — 20 kilometers

Lake Okeechobee

Lake Okeechobee is the second-largest freshwater lake in the United States. Only Lake Michigan is larger. *Okeechobee* means "big water" in the language of the Seminole, the local American-Indian tribe that originally named the lake. The body of water covers 4,730 square miles (1,891 sq km). Even so, it is shallow. On average, it is 9 feet (2.7 m) deep, but a person can easily wade in some areas.

HAMMOCKS, DOMES, AND HEADS

The Everglades is sometimes referred to as a marsh, a wetland where very few trees grow. In places where the limestone base rises higher in the marsh, even by just a few inches, hardwood hammocks, or tree islands, are formed. These hammocks seldom flood during the year. Instead, they remain dry because of their increased elevation. Many tropical plants grow in the protected hammocks, such as strangler fig, mahogany, gumbo-limbo, air plants, and ferns. White-tailed deer, bobcats, raccoons, and numerous other animal species make hardwood hammocks their home.

A hammock, or tree island, rises over the sawgrass prairie in the Everglades.

Cypress domes hold water year-round. These beautiful watery worlds are named after a prominent feature of the Everglades—dome-shaped **stands** of bald cypress. Cypress trees are conifers, meaning they have cones. They are not evergreens, however, because they lose their leaves once a year, during winter. In the winter months they look like bare twigs standing in water. The fallen leaves decay, creating a mild acid, which in turn dissolves the limestone. Over time, as more and more limestone is eaten away, the depressed areas deepen and widen into the pools we see today.

Small islands in the Everglades called heads occasionally become flooded. Heads are formed from decaying sawgrass and other plants that make **peat**. The type of tree growing on the head determines what it is called. Thus, willow and bay trees that take root in peat form willow heads and bay heads.

The center of a cypress dome is a wet world.

Taylor Slough remains full most of the year and supports much of the aquatic life in the Everglades.

LIFE-GIVING SLOUGHS AND MANGROVE FORESTS

Sloughs are another important part of the landscape in the Everglades. These depressions, or shallow cracks in the land, serve as the beds for slow-moving rivers or streams. A slough may contain the combination of freshwater and salt water known as **brackish water**. Sloughs are very important for water animals during the dry season, when most of the water in the Everglades drains out. In the sloughs, however, the water remains. The two main sloughs in the Everglades are Shark River Slough and Taylor Slough.

Mangrove forests lie at the lowest elevation in the Everglades. They are sometimes almost submerged in the brackish water that nourishes them. When the water level rises, sand and dirt are deposited around the mangrove trees' long, thin roots and create black soil.

Many animals live in the mangrove forests. A variety of fish and shrimp lay eggs among the trees' protective roots. Oysters and barnacles attach themselves to the roots, but raccoons, rats, and opossums pull them off for a quick snack. In fact, the so-called coon oyster, found among the mangroves, is the main food for raccoons.

Florida Bay is dotted by low mangrove islands called mangrove island keys. Also found in the bay are vast sea grass beds that are home to many marine animals. Manatees, stingrays, sharks, and sea turtles live in Florida Bay. In addition to being the most important breeding ground for wading birds in North America, Florida Bay is the only known area in which alligators and crocodiles live together.

◀ *A great blue heron wades among red mangroves.*

The Ten Thousand Islands are hundreds of mangrove islands that reach for 60 miles (97 km) along the Florida Gulf.

TEN THOUSAND ISLANDS

On the west side of the Everglades is a geographic feature known as the Ten Thousand Islands, which protect the Florida mainland from the floods, high winds, and waves that can accompany hurricanes. The islands attract hundreds of nesting birds such as ospreys and bald eagles. Swimming along the shores are silvery tarpon, which sometimes jump out of the water. There are also manatees, which dunk down to avoid passing boats. Most of these islands are mangrove islands, and in the low areas raccoons climb on tree branches as they scavenge for bird eggs.

Big Cypress Swamp Preserve

Bordering the northwest section of the Everglades is Big Cypress Swamp Preserve. This area covers 720,000 acres (291,374 ha). The region was set aside because the water flowing through Big Cypress is directly linked to Everglades National Park. Freshwater flows through the massive cypress domes and empties into the Ten Thousand Islands area.

Big Cypress is called a preserve because its laws are not as strict as those regulating a national park. A preserve allows cattle grazing, oil exploration, and air boats, also called swamp buggies. There is a hunting season for deer and turkey every fall.

The Ten Thousand Islands are surrounded by water of all types—salt, brackish, and fresh. It is easy to identify the type of water because saltwater islands have oyster beds that become exposed during low tide. As the water becomes fresher, vegetation on the islands changes, and palm and cypress trees can be seen.

EVERGLADES SEASONS

On a world map, South Florida is in the Desert Belt, which means it is at the same latitude as the Sahara and Arabian deserts. Because Florida is surrounded by water on three sides, the environment in much of the state is moist and humid.

Heavy rains are typical during the wet season, from May through October. Rain showers are often accompanied by dramatic and loud thunderstorms. Rainfall averages about 60 inches (150 cm) per year. During the wet season, the Everglades is expected to fill with water. In years with below-average rainfall, this does not happen, and crippling drought sometimes results.

The average temperature in the wet season is 90 degrees Fahrenheit (32 degrees Celsius) with humidity up to 90 percent. Because of these hot, moist conditions, mosquitoes swarm freshwater lakes and any passing visitors. The hurricane season (June–November) lies mainly in the wet months.

Florida is in an area known as the Hurricane Belt, and indeed the Everglades has been hit by many hurricanes. Plants and animals living in the Everglades have evolved over thousands of years to

Bare trees are all that is left after a hurricane pounded the Everglades.

survive these high-wind storms. Most of the plants grow low to the ground. Even the main resident, the alligator, has a low-lying body.

During the dry season (November–April), water is absorbed into the ground or slowly empties into Florida Bay. The temperature in the park ranges from 77 °F (25 °C) to 53 °F (12 °C). There have been instances of temperatures dropping to almost 40 °F (4.4 °C) during the dry season, but such near-freezing periods are extremely rare.

Everglades National Park and Hurricanes

In 1992 Hurricane Andrew caused tremendous amounts of damage in the Everglades. It ripped up the boardwalks and other displays of the park. It also tore through Homestead, a town bordering the park, and forced more than 250,000 people to evacuate their homes. Homestead Air Force Base was destroyed by winds exceeding 175 miles (281 km) per hour.

Thirteen years later, in 2005, Hurricane Wilma surged into the Everglades and tore up two areas that contained roseate spoonbill nesting colonies. Hurricanes Wilma and Katrina destroyed the park's Flamingo Lodge, Visitor Center, and restaurant. The storms dumped several inches of mud in the lodge, cabin, and docking areas.

THREE

Unusual Plants and Animals

The plants and animals of the Everglades are an unusual blend. This is because South Florida has a temperate, or mild, climate in addition to the subtropical weather it is famous for. Subtropical environments support animals and plants as diverse as loggerhead turtles, crocodiles, flamingos, and air plants. Temperate environments include northern animals and plants such as bobcats, white-tailed deer, raccoons, and pine trees.

BIRDS, BIRDS, AND MORE BIRDS

More than 360 species of birds visit or live in the Everglades. Some are wading birds, which formerly blanketed the area in immense swarms. Today, 90 to 95 percent of the wading bird population has disappeared.

The Everglades hosts a wide variety of animals, especially birds such as this brown pelican.

WADING BIRDS

In the early 1900s wading birds were killed in huge numbers for the beautiful **plumes** that were used to decorate ladies' hats. Later, poor water management practices, such as the building of dikes and canals in the Everglades, also caused the wading birds to die. When water from the vast wetlands was funneled into the dikes and canals, the wading birds' habitat dried up and could no longer support large populations. One of the main reasons Everglades National Park was formed was to protect the area from any further loss of bird species.

Within the Everglades are green-backed heron, Louisiana heron, yellow-crowned night heron, black-crowned night heron, tricolored heron, and other heron species. The great blue heron is the largest wading bird in North America. It can stand up to 4 feet (1.2 m) tall with its neck extended. Its wingspan is almost 6 feet (1.8 m).

The great blue heron's large, bowl-shaped nest is made of sticks and grass. The bird eats small mammals along with fish and frogs. While hunting, the great blue heron stands motionless and then quickly snatches its prey in its long, strong beak.

The little blue heron, which stands only 22 inches (56 cm) tall, strikes with lightning-fast speed. It lives in fresh- and saltwater areas of the Everglades and can be found close to the water's edge or wading through shallow water searching for food.

A beautiful pink bird that can be seen during the winter months in the Everglades is the roseate spoonbill, with its characteristic

Great blue herons watch over their new hatchling.

spoon-shaped beak that measures about 6 inches (15 cm) long. To feed, it stands in shallow water and moves its bill back and forth as it trolls for small fish and shrimp.

Other Everglades wading birds are white ibises, wood storks, great egrets, and snowy white egrets. Although now a protected species, the white ibis was at one time known as the Chokoloskee chicken because it was eaten by early residents of the Everglades. The snowy white egret almost became extinct in the 1920s because of overhunting. Its long, white feathers were perfect for decorating hats and making elegant fans. Now an endangered animal, the snowy white egret is protected by law.

Another water bird is the anhinga, also called the snake bird because of its long neck and scalelike feathers, and the water turkey because of its fan-shaped tail. The anhinga has a sharp-

The beauty of the anhinga's plumage can be seen when it dries itself in the Florida sun.

pointed beak that is used to stab fish at mealtime. After running a fish through with its beak, the anhinga throws the prey into the air, grabs it headfirst, and swallows. Even though the anhinga is a water bird, its feathers do not have oil to help keep its feathers dry. Instead, after swimming, the anhinga must extend its wings in the sun to dry them off.

A visitor to the Everglades is the brilliant pink flamingo. It travels all the way from the Caribbean Sea. Flocks can sometimes be seen wading in Florida Bay at different times during the year.

OTHER EVERGLADES BIRDS

One of the largest birds in southern Florida is the white pelican. Its wingspan can reach up to 9 feet (2.7 m). Flocks of white pelican sometimes catch wind currents and soar high in the sky.

Nonwading Everglades birds include ospreys, which have a whistling call, turkey vultures, which can sometimes be spotted perched atop a tree in a cypress dome, and bald eagles. There are about fifty pairs of bald eagles nesting in the Everglades. They mainly eat small reptiles and mammals and nest in the keys of Florida Bay, in the mangroves, and in the pinelands.

Small screech owls can sometimes be seen nesting in hardwood hammocks. These birds have even been known to occupy the abandoned nests of woodpeckers. They eat insects, small birds, and mice.

An extremely rare bird, which lives only in the Everglades, is the

Everglades kite. Its diet consists only of apple snails. Another bird dependent on apple snails is the limpkin. Not strong flyers, limpkins have a very limited flight range. The name is derived from the creatures' awkward, limplike walk.

MAMMALS

Within the Everglades there are forty different mammalian species. Animals that live on hammocks are white-tailed deer, black bears, bobcats, raccoons, opossums, marsh rabbits, and Florida panthers. The small marsh rabbit feeds on the various grasses that grow in the Everglades. Its fur is brown with black, and its ears are tiny and round.

◀ *The limpkin's long bill is perfect for foraging for its favorite meal, apple snails.*

Florida's State Mammal

The Florida panther, Florida's state mammal since 1982, can grow to a length of almost 7 feet (2 m). Its body is large, and its tail is long. Its fur is a tawny color.

The natural behavior of the Florida panther is to roam a large territory while hunting white-tailed deer, its main food source. Sightings of Florida panthers are rare in Big Cypress National Preserve and in Everglades National Park. Environmentalists believe that there are only about thirty to fifty Florida panthers living in the wild, and the animals have been listed as endangered since 1967.

White-tailed deer, an incredibly fast and agile prey species, are found in Big Cypress National Preserve and Everglades National Park. The male's head is adorned with antlers, which are shed every year. These tawny-furred deer can sometimes be spotted in pinelands, on Long Pine Key, and in Shark Valley.

Tree snails thrive in warm, wet climates.

SNAILS AND BUGS

The Everglades is home to many small creatures. During the wet season, tree snails can be found feeding on the **lichen** that grow on tree bark. Their shells reach an adult size of 2 to 3 inches (5 to 8 cm) and have black, yellow, or white stripes. During the dry season, these snails **estivate**, or sleep, until the rainy season begins.

Among the spiders that live in the Everglades is the jumping spider. Instead of spinning a web to catch its food, it hunts its prey on foot. The fishing spider makes a web underwater and catches small fish in it. The crab spider was given its name because it walks like a crab. The black scorpion, a spiderlike creature of the Everglades, can give a nasty bite.

Beautiful butterflies also live in the Everglades: the gold and blue monarch butterfly, the black and white spicebush swallowtail, and the buckeye butterfly, which is colored brown, white, and red.

The Everglades host several butterfly species, including the buckeye butterfly.

REPTILES

There are over fifty types of reptiles in the Everglades. The most common species, the American alligator, is represented in Florida by thousands of individuals living in fresh and brackish water. The largest recorded American alligator in Florida was 17 feet 5 inches (5.3 m) long. However, the majority of alligators are between 9 and 11 feet (2.7 and 3.4 m) long.

Female alligators are very protective of their young. They build mound-shaped nests ranging from 7 to 10 feet (2.1 to 3 m) in diameter and 2 to 3 feet (0.6 to 0.9 m) high. Alligators lay thirty-five to fifty eggs that they then cover with sawgrass. Upon hatching, the

The American alligator is the most common reptile found in the Everglades.

baby alligators make a high-pitched call. When the mother alligator hears it, she tears the sawgrass cover off so the hatchlings can come out of the nest. Alligators are 6 to 8 inches (15 to 20 cm) long when first hatched. Alligator mothers do not feed their young. However, they do protect them for up to two years.

The Everglades is the only place where alligators and crocodiles live side by side. There are about 500 to 1,200 endangered American crocodiles living in Florida in brackish or salty water. These huge reptiles are much more likely to attack a human than are American alligators. American crocodiles can grow up to 15 feet (4.6 m) long. Their teeth are visible outside their snout, and their skin is grayish. The crocodile has a snout that is much smaller, narrower, and more pointed than that of the alligator.

Alligator Holes

Alligators are constantly searching for water in the Everglades, especially during the dry season. They can sense water close to the earth's surface even though the sources cannot be seen. To get to the water, an alligator uses its thick, strong tail and clawed feet to break the dry mud. With its long snout, it shovels away twigs and other debris. During times of severe drought, it is not unheard of for alligators to dig down 4 feet (1.2 m). As they dig deeper and deeper, water seeps into the holes they have made. Once water has filled the hole, it attracts other animals searching for water. Sometimes, these animals become alligator meals!

As time goes by, alligator holes develop into distinct ecosystems with fish and insects. Plants such as cattail, water lily, and bladderwort begin growing there. Herons and other birds come to feed on the fish and insects. The rainy season eventually returns, and the animals disperse. But during dry, waterless times in the Everglades, alligator holes keep the cycle of life continuing.

Florida water snakes, Everglades rat snakes, rough green snakes, scarlet snakes, and corn snakes are among the many snakes that thrive in the warm, moist environment of the Everglades. The corn snake is a constrictor. It squeezes its prey before swallowing it whole. The longest native snake, the Eastern indigo snake, can grow to almost 9 feet (2.7 m) long. Four snakes in the Everglades are venomous. They are the pygmy rattlesnake, the diamondback rattlesnake, the cottonmouth moccasin, and the coral snake.

A rough green snake blends into its natural surroundings.

Largest Non-native Snake

Burmese pythons, which can reach lengths exceeding 23 feet (7 m), were introduced into the Everglades in an uncontrolled way. They were abandoned there by people who had acquired them as pets. Because they are so huge, pythons have been known to attempt to eat alligators.

In 2005 park staff discovered a gruesome sight. A Burmese python had constricted and swallowed a 6-foot (1.8-m) alligator, but the alligator had clawed its way out of the snake's belly. Both reptiles died during the struggle.

Scientists are very concerned about the growing number of pythons living in the Everglades. The alligator has always been the top predator there. But now with the python, two reptile species are fighting for the title of top predator. Scientists want to rid the Everglades of the python, and over 150 pythons have been caught and removed by park staff.

A variety of turtles live in the Everglades. In freshwater ponds, marshes, and sloughs are Florida softshell turtles, which can stay underwater for long periods of time. There are also Florida red-belly turtles, Florida sliders, striped mud turtles, and Florida snapping turtles. The pinelands, hammocks, and other land areas provide habitat for box turtles. In the coastal waters of Florida Bay, there are loggerhead turtles, leatherbacks, and hawksbills.

Tree frogs are found throughout the Everglades.

Also living in the hammocks are tree frogs, such as the green tree frog. To easily climb over vegetation, the green tree frog has toes like suction cups. In freshwater marshes are pig frogs, whose loud grunts can be heard day and night.

Fish

A huge variety of fish can be found in the Everglades. Many sports enthusiasts visit this national park to fish for largemouth bass and tarpon. Sunfish, bream, garfish, and tiny mosquito fish are abundant.

Because of the wet and dry seasons of the Everglades, sometimes fish find themselves in shrinking ponds

Manatees

A large mammal that swims in the freshwater rivers and lakes as well as the salty water of Florida Bay is the manatee. A manatee's skin is grayish brown, sometimes speckled green with algae. The front flippers are used to steer as the gentle giants push through the water with their large, flat tails. Manatee adults can weigh 800 to 1,200 pounds (362 to 544 kilograms) and can reach lengths of over 9 feet (3 m). To support their massive weight, they have to eat about 200 pounds (90 kg) of vegetation a day. Sea grass is a main food source.

of water. Fish such as bass, bream, and sunfish die when the water level becomes too low. However, some fish have learned to adapt to these changes. Mosquito fish, garfish, and bowfin have either evolved lungs or developed survival techniques to stay alive in mud.

Plants

One of the most common plants in the Everglades is sawgrass, named for the pointed notches, like the teeth of a saw, on its spiny leaves. Even the plant's petals are spiky. Walking through dense sawgrass growth feels like walking through shards of glass. Sawgrass can grow up to 10 feet (3 m) high. This extremely tough plant cannot be flattened by any natural force short of hurricane winds.

Sawgrass is a sturdy, spiny plant that grows in abundance in the Everglades.

Surprisingly, sawgrass is not a grass at all. It is a member of the **sedge** family—stiff, grasslike plants that usually grow in wet ground or water. Sedge is among the oldest plants on Earth.

Another unusual plant is the slash pine. Its moist, thick bark is spongy like cork, and this property protects the tree during forest fires. The occasional forest fire actually helps the slash pine multiply. This is because slash pines can survive a fire that destroys competing vegetation.

Other trees found in the park are the custard apple tree, buttonwood, wax myrtle, wild coffee, and satinleaf. An unusual tree is the strangler fig. It plants its seeds on other trees called host trees. When the seeds begin to grow, the strangler fig's roots drop to the ground, where they wrap around the trunk of the host tree and eventually kill it.

A strangler fig grows along the outside of a tree in the Everglades.

The gumbo-limbo tree has red bark that peels off its trunk. Because it reminds people of a tourist with a peeling sunburn, locals call it the tourist tree.

There are four types of mangrove in the Everglades: red, white, buttonwood, and black. Mangroves can grow as tall as 80 feet (24 m). They are supported by roots called props, which grow from their trunks.

Black mangroves have unusual root systems. Their main roots grow buried deep in seawater or mud. Additional roots, which rise from the water into the air, prevent the tree from drowning. These half-inch (1.3-cm) roots provide the black mangrove with much-needed oxygen.

The Importance of Periphyton

Floating in the water of the Everglades are yellowish slimy clumps called periphyton. Periphyton is an important food source consisting of hundreds of different types of algae. It nourishes small water animals at the bottom of the food chain, including snails, insects, small fish, and shrimp. During the dry season, periphyton becomes crumbly. Even when it seems dry, however, it is a source of water. Thus, fish eggs and other small marine creatures live in periphyton until the rains come again.

What Is an Air Plant?

Instead of having its roots in dirt, an air plant absorbs nourishment through its leaves. Its food consists of nutrients in the dust and other airborne particles. Air plants do not require much water, but they also do not mind a lot of water. In addition, they do not need direct sunlight to grow.

An air plant that is related to the pineapple is the stiff-leaved wild pine. The largest air plant, the giant wild pine, can reach widths of up to 4 feet (1.2 m). After a rain, small pools of water may form in its cup-shaped leaves. These pools are excellent places for little lizards to get a drink.

FLOWERS

Many flowers grow in the Everglades: white water lilies and swamp lilies in water holes, blue and purple morning glories on trees or vines. Near the sandy coast are firewheels, which have orange petals with yellow tips.

Some of the most beautiful Everglades flowers are orchids, which are considered to be air plants. Unlike the firewheels and morning glories, orchids prefer darker environments such as hardwood hammocks or cypress domes. Butterfly orchids, with petals shaped like butterfly wings, look as though they are suspended in air.

Butterfly orchids are some of the many flowering plants in the Everglades.

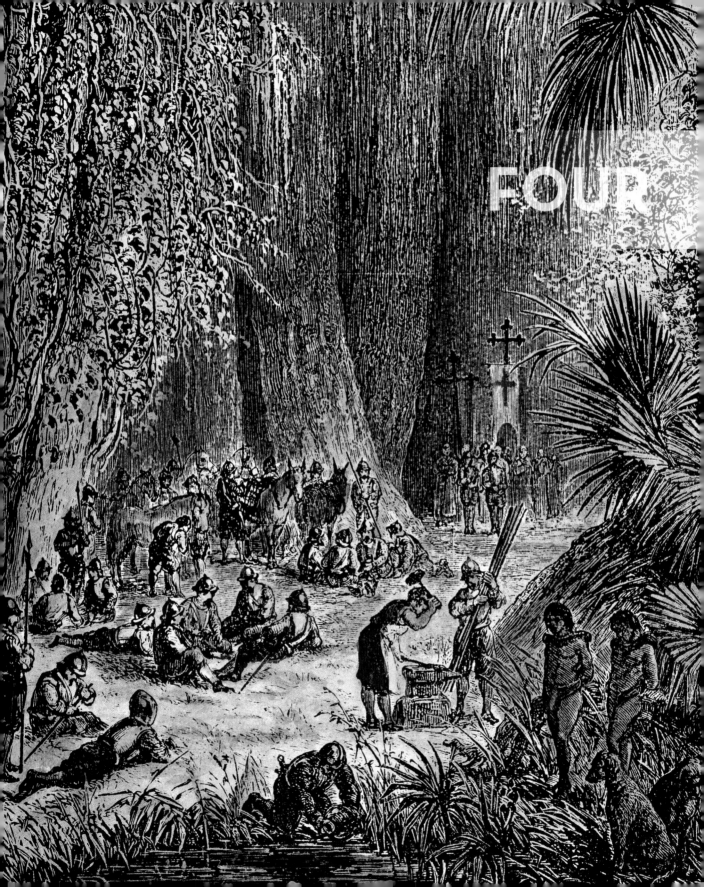

FOUR

History Reshapes the Everglades

Humans have inhabited the region of the Everglades for about 12,000 years. American Indians of the Calusa and Tequesta tribes were living in the Everglades when the area was discovered by Europeans in the 1500s.

EVERGLADES FIRST INHABITANTS

The Calusa resided in the southwest section of the Everglades near present-day Everglades City. They cleared canals through the marshlands and used them like roads for their dugout canoes.

The Calusa had a structured social system. A chief led the tribe with complete authority. The word *Calusa* means "fierce people," and these ferocious, well-organized warriors dominated the majority of American-Indian tribes living in southern Florida.

The Calusa had an abundant food supply of clams, oysters, conch, and other shellfish. The huge shell garbage mounds they left are

The Spanish, who arrived to explore the region that is now Florida as early as 1513, changed the course of the area's history.

The first peoples of the Everglades used dugout canoes to travel through the canals.

similar to modern-day dumps. Some of these mounds formed entire islands in the Ten Thousand Islands near Everglades City.

Because they did not have to worry about food constantly, the Calusa were able to develop aspects of culture that were important to them, such as religion and art. In their religious festivals, they wore fearsome masks shaped like alligator or panther heads. They also made toys and jewelry from shells and wood.

The Tequesta lived on the southeast side of the Everglades at modern-day Biscayne Bay, south of Miami. These expert fishermen used ropes and pointed stakes to catch manatees, stingrays, and large ocean fish, including sharks.

Both the Calusa and the Tequesta knew how to use the many natural resources of the Everglades. They built canoes out of cypress trunks and used wood, sharks' teeth, and shells to make weapons and tools.

THE SPANISH

Under the leadership of Juan Ponce de León, the Spanish arrived on the Florida peninsula in 1513. De León had come to the New World with Christopher Columbus and was known as an explorer and adventurer. He immediately claimed the mainland territory for himself and named it La Florida, or "Feast of the Flowers."

Because de León and his men had numerous battles with the Calusa, the Europeans never settled in Florida. Instead, after their leader was severely wounded by a Calusa arrow, they withdrew to Havana, Cuba, where de Léon died in 1521.

Juan Ponce de León and his men explore the region he named La Florida, or "Feast of the Flowers."

Once news of the discovery of Florida reached Spain, the Spanish began arriving in large numbers. They quickly built forts and missions. The Calusa fought the invaders for hundreds of years, and over time, these battles took a heavy toll on the American Indians. In addition, the Europeans brought diseases, such as smallpox and

Thatched shelters stand in a Seminole village in the Everglades.

measles, which killed huge numbers of native peoples in Florida and elsewhere. When the Spanish arrived, there had been about 20,000 American Indians living in South Florida. By the mid-seventeenth century, the number of Calusa and Tequesta had diminished to just several hundred.

Some of the Tequesta converted to Christianity in response to the efforts of Spanish missionaries. A Roman Catholic mission and a church were built to serve the growing number of converts.

In 1763 Spain **ceded** Florida to Great Britain. By this time, there

were very few American Indians left in South Florida. The British found all the American Indians had gone to Cuba with the Spanish.

THE SEMINOLE

In the 1800s American Indians from Georgia and Alabama moved to the Everglades. They were under pressure from the U.S. government to yield land in the two southern states to white settlers. These American Indians were known as the Seminole, meaning "wild people" or "runaway."

The Seminole were farmers. They grew crops, raised livestock such as cattle and pigs, and sold animal hides. They also allowed black runaway slaves to live with them. These slaves often became tribesmen.

THE SEMINOLE WARS

Once the Seminole had settled in Florida, they had several skirmishes with white settlers and the U.S. Army. There were battles over cattle and over demands for slaves to be returned. The initial conflicts between the Seminole and the white settlers, from 1817 to 1818, are known as the First Seminole War. Pockets of resistance remained.

Fighting between the Seminole and the settlers did not stop until 1832, when a small number of Seminole in South Florida signed a treaty that required all Seminole to give up their land in Florida and move west to Oklahoma. The migration was intended to further a policy of President Andrew Jackson, enacted by Congress as the Indian Removal Act of 1830. Some Seminole left, but others refused and escaped to the no-man's-land of the Everglades. The Seminole who stayed began the Second Seminole War. Another tribe, the Miccosukee, joined the Seminole to help them fight. The Second Seminole War lasted from 1835 to 1842. After nearly a generation of peace, another battle began because of land disputes between white settlers and the remaining Seminole. The Conflict stretched from 1855 to 1858.

Osceola: A Seminole Leader

One of the most famous American-Indian leaders during the Seminole Wars was Osceola. Even though he was not officially a chief, he acted like one. His thin, muscular frame and his fiery eyes captivated his fellow tribesmen. Osceola refused to leave the Everglades and insisted that his people stay with him. Because of his passion, he was  able to lead other Seminole warriors against the U.S. Army for about two years. In 1837, however, he was captured and imprisoned. Osceola died of a throat infection acquired in prison.

Fighting wars in the unfriendly Everglades was brutal work for the U.S. soldiers. Because the water in the streams and canals was so shallow, they often had to drag their canoes, which were laden with rifles and provisions. The sharp sawgrass cut their skin, and swarms of mosquitoes attacked, spreading diseases such as malaria and yellow fever. Many of the troops died, not from battle wounds, but from the horrible conditions and exposure in the Everglades.

U.S. troops navigate the Everglades under the watchful eyes of the Seminole during the Seminole Wars.

The Seminole, however, had adapted to life in the river of grass. They established small camps on hardwood hammocks. Their main food was fresh fish and game, supplemented by cabbage palm and coontie, a starchy plant. Because of their superior Everglades survival skills, they won battle after battle.

In 1858, after years of fighting at a cost of millions of dollars, the U.S. Army gave up and abandoned the Seminole Wars. These battles were also costly in terms of human life. Thousands of American Indians, black slaves, and troops in the U.S. Army and U.S. Navy had died. At this time, there were only two hundred to three hundred

American Indians left in the region. They stayed in the territory they had successfully defended and settled in Big Cypress Swamp and the western Everglades.

Today, the Seminole and their Miccosukee allies are the only American-Indian tribes remaining in the Everglades. In 1957 the Seminole tribe gained federal status as the Seminole Tribe of Florida. The Miccosukee received federal recognition in 1962.

OTHER SETTLERS IN THE EVERGLADES

From the mid-1800s to the early 1900s, white settlers attempted to establish small towns in the Everglades. One such settlement was Flamingo, located at the tip of Florida and founded in 1893. The few families who made Flamingo their home lived by farming, fishing, and hunting. Today, Flamingo is part of Everglades National Park.

THE DIMINISHING EVERGLADES

Even as early as the 1830s, some government officials knew that the uninhabitable area of southern Florida would one day be used for agriculture. They knew the first step would be to drain the Everglades of its water. Then sugar, citrus fruit, and a variety of vegetables could be planted to supply food for the growing U.S. population. The process began when Congress ordered a survey of the Everglades for the purpose of developing a plan to drain the area.

A plan in the 1920s was devised to stop the natural water flow of the Everglades because of devastating flooding. A huge dike or wall was built around Lake Okeechobee to prevent water from flooding the surrounding communities and farmlands. When the lake was about to overflow, the doors in the walls of the dike were opened, allowing water to surge into the canals that led to the Atlantic Ocean. This diversion of water slowly began to dry up the Everglades.

Building the Tamiami Trail

In the 1920s construction began on a road that cuts directly across the natural southward flow of the Everglades from Lake Okeechobee. It was the east-west segment of the Tamiami Trail, an engineering marvel of its time, which connects Tampa, Florida, on the Gulf of Mexico, to Miami, on the Atlantic Ocean. Directed by Seminole Indian guides, inmates from the state prison cut through the thick underbrush growing in shallow water and made a clearing 100 feet (30 m) wide. Other workmen were employed to handle the next phase. They used over 2.5 million sticks of dynamite to blast through the limestone that was used as fill for the road. This created two canals, one on either side of the Tamiami Trail. Oxcarts and modern machinery pulled dynamite and other supplies through the muck. This 273-mile (439-km) road was completed in April 1928, and it changed the natural landscape of the Everglades forever.

Also during the 1920s, South Florida began to boom. Towns like Miami and Fort Lauderdale grew quickly. Stores, hotels, and other businesses were built. Tourists such as fishermen, sports hunters, and yachters came in droves. Roads were constructed and canals were dug to make the area more livable. Freight trains coming into Miami were filled with roofing, windows, nails, and other construction materials. Millions of dollars were poured into huge hotels on Miami Beach. Mangrove forests were ripped out to allow uninterrupted ocean views.

The 1920s was a time of great growth in Miami.

An even bigger change to the Everglades' natural water flow began in 1948, when Congress approved a project intended to place canals and **levees** across South Florida. The **U.S. Army Corps of Engineers** was assigned to get the job done. By contructing canals and levees, the government hoped to ensure that cities, towns, and farmers would have enough water. An additional goal was to make sure the Everglades remained protected.

Once the canals and levees were in place, 50 percent of all wetlands in South Florida disappeared. The man-made ebb and flow of water to the Everglades began to severely damage the region's wildlife. A population explosion in South Florida also put more and more pressure on water resources.

Even though the Everglades had been declared a protected area, these changes resulted in the disappearance of huge flocks of wading birds. Many other animals also died as their habitat changed. The landscape of the Everglades would never be the same.

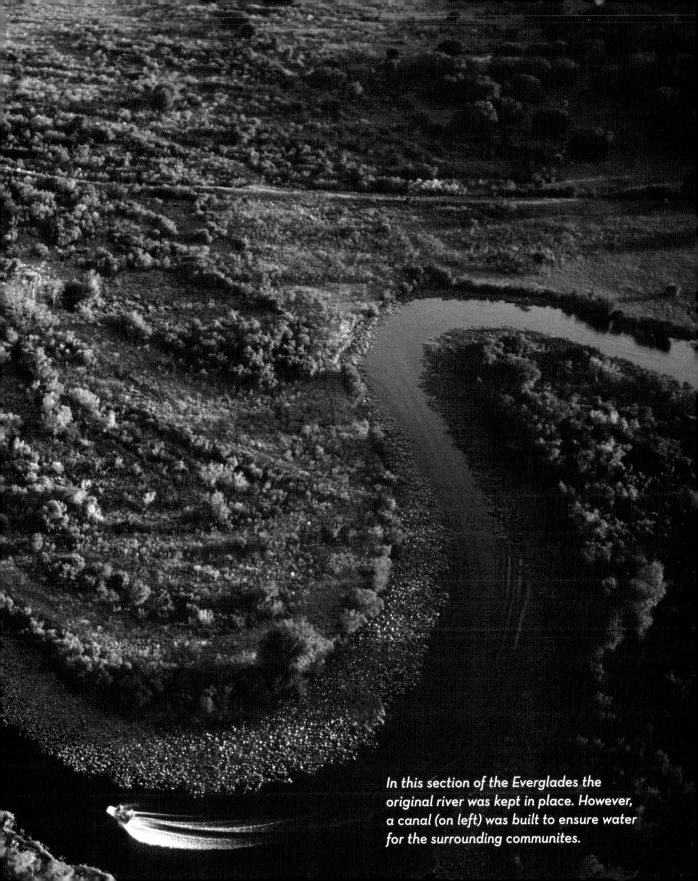

In this section of the Everglades the original river was kept in place. However, a canal (on left) was built to ensure water for the surrounding communites.

FIVE

Living in and around the Everglades

The only people allowed to live within the boundaries of the Everglades are the Miccosukee and the Seminole Indians. Their name for the Everglades is Pa-hay-okee, or "Grassy Water," and they have lived there for almost two hundred years. The Miccosukee and Seminole people currently living on reservations in Florida are descendants of the determined American Indians who remained in the Everglades during the Seminole Wars.

THE MICCOSUKEE

Today, there are three established Miccosukee reservations in Florida. On the northern border of Everglades National Park is the Miccosukee Tribal Headquarters. The center of the Miccosukee population, however, is located on the Tamiami Trail Reservation, site of the Miccosukee Information Center and Indian Village. Visitors are welcome to tour the village and to get a glimpse of the

◀ *A family enjoys their time together at the Miccosukee Tribal School.*

A Miccosukee woman displays her beadwork at the tribe's annual arts festival.

history of the tribe. In addition, a variety of Miccosukee crafts, such as dolls, baskets, and wood carvings, are sold.

Alligator Alley Reservation, south of the Everglades Parkway, also called Alligator Alley, covers 74,812 acres (30,275 ha), making it the largest reservation. The Krome Avenue Reservation, near Miami, features a gambling casino.

The Miccosukee tribal government, the Miccosukee General

Council, includes a court system and a police department. The tribe also operates modern schools and daycare and senior centers. All these facilities incorporate traditional Indian ways as well as more modern approaches.

While visiting the Everglades, you may see buildings called chickees, the traditional Miccosukee homes. The palm-frond roofs held up by cypress poles are familiar sights to people driving along the Tamiami Trail and elsewhere in South Florida. Some Miccosukee still live in chickees, but most live in modern houses. Today, there are about 550 Miccosukee living in the tribe's reservation system.

The Clans of the Miccosukee

The Miccosukee are separated into groups of families from the same ancestor. Each such group, or clan, has an identifying name. Some Miccosukee clan names are as follows:

Koowe	Panther clan
Fooshe	Bird clan
Oshane	Otter clan
Eeche	Deer clan

A chickee's roof is constructed with palm fronds.

THE SEMINOLE

Similar to the Miccosukee, the Seminole have a tribal government. There are six different Seminole Reservations in Florida. The Big Cypress Reservation, in western Florida, on both sides of Alligator Alley, is home to the Ah-Tah-Thi-Ki Museum. The museum displays illustrate the history of the Seminole. Big Cypress has a living village as well.

The Seminole own huge gambling businesses. The Hollywood Reservation, along the east side of the Tamiami Trail, is famous as the site of the Seminole Hard Rock Hotel and Casino. The tribal headquarters are also located on the Hollywood Reservation.

In addition, the Seminole are involved in agriculture, and several citrus farms can be found on the Brighton Reservation located on the northwest shore of Lake Okeechobee.

TOWNS BORDERING THE EVERGLADES

Just outside the northwestern corner of Everglades National Park is Everglades City. Founded in 1864, this city was originally slated to become the business and government center of Collier County. But, on September 10, 1960, Everglades City was hit by a devastating storm, Hurricane Donna. The entire town was leveled. After the hurricane, the government center of Collier County was established in Naples, 35 miles (56 km) to the north.

Today, Everglades City's main industry is stone crabbing. Many of the locals either own a crabbing boat or work for someone who does. Game fishing and air-boat tours offer other employment opportunities for residents of one of Florida's least prosperous municipalities.

About 5 miles (8 km) outside Everglades City lies Chokoloskee, a small island separated from the mainland by a causeway. The island has an area of about 150 acres (60 ha).

Before the arrival of the Spanish, Chokoloskee was occupied by the Calusa, who built palm-thatched homes and left shellfish garbage mounds. Today, shells can be found on the ground throughout the island.

The island's small town, also called Chokoloskee, was first occupied by white settlers in the 1870s. In 1906 Ted Smallwood built a

Grandmother of the Glades

Born on April 7, 1890, in Minneapolis, Minnesota, Marjory Stoneman Douglas moved to Miami, Florida, when she was twenty-five years old. As an assistant editor for the *Miami Herald* she began to write about Florida's unusual landscape, including the Everglades. At this time, the Everglades had not been set aside as a national park. Douglas was among the first to understand the importance of saving this unique area.

In 1947 Douglas wrote and published *The Everglades: River of Grass.* The book introduced thousands of readers to the Everglades. As a result, people began to develop an appreciation of the fragile and beautiful Glades environment.

In 1969, at nearly eighty years old, she founded the Friends of the Everglades which fought to close the drainage canals, save the endangered species of the Everglades, and implement limitations on farming and real estate development. Their activities, along with those of other groups trying the save the Everglades, have been widely praised.

This true friend of the Everglades died on May 14, 1998, at 108 years of age. Her body was cremated, and her remains were scattered over the Everglades.

trading post, which is a museum today. During the early 1900s, the Seminole came to the trading post to exchange hides and furs for money or supplies. Smallwood became their personal banker, holding the Seminole's silver coins in a wooden box inside the building. Ernest F. Coe was known to visit the trading post.

Located on the northeastern border of Everglades National Park are two farming communities, Homestead and Florida City. Because they are right next to each other, they share a chamber of commerce. These two towns were founded in the early 1900s. In the center of Homestead is a historical area with several landmarks. There are modern stores and services in this area, but some of the buildings have been boarded up. The destruction of Homestead Air Force Base during Hurricane Andrew resulted in the loss of many local businesses.

Agriculture is the main industry in this area. Southern Florida grows almost half the winter vegetables eaten in the United States. Some major crops are mango, cucumber, squash, and avocado.

People from Spanish-speaking countries flock to Homestead and Florida City to pick crops. Many business signs are in Spanish. Several restaurants and bakeries offer Hispanic specialties.

TOURISM

In 2007 the number of tourists visiting Everglades National Park was 1,074,764. Access to the park area is almost unrestricted. People can stop anywhere along the main roads and hike out into the grasslands,

Father of Everglades National Park

Ernest F. Coe was born in 1866 in New Haven, Connecticut. He graduated from Yale University's School of Fine Arts in 1887 and moved to the Miami area in 1925. His love of nature took him to the Everglades. From his explorations, he soon realized that the habitat was in serious trouble. Orchids were being removed, and rare birds were being slaughtered.

In 1928, to help protect the area, Coe formed an organization called the Tropical Everglades National Park Association. He worked very hard to get the Everglades recognized as a national park. In a letter to the director of the National Park Service, he proposed that the southern tip of Florida be set aside for that purpose.

Officials in Washington, D.C., became interested and sent an inspection party, which included Marjory Stoneman Douglas. These early environmentalists chose the area that is now Everglades National Park. Many years passed before the park became a reality, and within four years of the 1947 dedication ceremony, Ernest F. Coe died.

To commemorate his contributions to the region, Everglades National Park opened the Ernest F. Coe Visitor Center in 1996.

Agricultural workers from Spanish-speaking countries work on many of the farms in Homestead, Florida.

a practice called slogging. An old pair of tennis shoes, long pants, and long-sleeved shirts provide important protection from the saw-grass. In many areas, tourists can walk out to a cypress dome, where they will enter a green world full of air plants and orchids.

EVERGLADES TRAILS AND DISPLAYS

The National Park Service has constructed several stops to enhance visitors' experience of the park and all its wonders. The majority of stops and the largest visitor center are located on the east side of Everglades National Park, close to Homestead.

At the park's entrance is the Ernest F. Coe Visitor Center. Once inside, one hears the sounds of frogs croaking and alligators bellowing. These special effects come from informative displays inside the center.

The road from the east entrance wanders down to Florida Bay and ends in Flamingo. Although most of the facilities were destroyed or severely damaged by hurricanes Katrina and Wilma in 2005, many boaters still come to Flamingo to fish out of Florida Bay. Even while standing on the shore, visitors can actually see fish jumping out of the water.

◀◀ *A tour guide points out a place of interest along the Anhinga Trail at the Royal Palms Visitors Center.*

Sometimes American crocodiles can be spotted on the banks, and manatees swimming next to the docks. Small boats such as canoes and skiffs can be rented. Some visitors, however, prefer to sign up for the guided back-country tour, which departs from the dock.

Farther up the road toward the park entrance are Coot Bay Pond and Mazarek Pond. The water at Coot Bay is chocolate brown from the many mangroves. In the middle of Mazarek Pond, tourists might see dragonflies hovering around a swimming alligator.

The next stop is West Lake Trail, which is completely silent. This boardwalk weaves in and out of a mangrove forest. A smell of rotten eggs hangs in the air because of hydrogen sulfide gas released by decomposing plants. This trail circles around to views of West Lake, which seems to expand endlessly to the east. Further down the road is the Pineland Trail. It is a long boardwalk that winds through tree islands.

The most popular stop along the road from the east entrance is Royal Palm, which gives access to the Anhinga Trail. Depending on the season, visitors walking along the boardwalk can spot alligators, anhingas, cormorants, and turtles in the slough. The other trail at Royal Palm is the Gumbo-Limbo Trail, which looks like a jungle because of the thick green plants.

Outside the east entrance to the park, along the Tamiami Trail road, is Shark Valley. A tram ride takes visitors through the valley, which is named after the deep Shark Valley Slough. This slough attracts a variety of wildlife such as alligators, blue and white herons, anhingas, roseate spoonbills, and large snapping turtles.

The west section of the park mainly consists of mangrove islands, the famous Ten Thousand Islands. Boat tours depart from the dock to take visitors out to the islands. Tourists will see a variety of birds, and sometimes a bottlenose dolphin will follow a boat's wake.

SIX

Saving the Everglades

People have changed the Everglades. The huge volume of families and individuals moving to South Florida has gradually choked the slow-moving river. Vast agricultural fields, freeways, housing developments, universities, and corporate headquarters surround the Everglades. In addition to the 6 million residents who call South Florida home, around 30 million tourists visit the area every year. Retirement communities, golf courses, malls, sports fishing, and yachting are just some of the attractions.

What's left of the Everglades is slowly dying. The Everglades relies on water flowing from Lake Okeechobee, but the lake has been dammed several times. Today, less and less freshwater makes its way to the Everglades. Instead, salt water is encroaching inland. The abundance of salt water is unbalancing the region's sensitive ecosystem. Estuaries—bodies of water in which the sea meets freshwater—are no longer supporting their unique plants and animals. This is because less freshwater is flowing into them.

◄ *Preserving the natural beauty and wildlife of the Everglades is an endeavor taken on by many who realize the importance of this wonder of nature.*

This housing development was built on reclaimed lands of the Everglades.

Water pollution is another condition destroying the Everglades. One of the biggest polluters is **phosphorus**, which is commonly found in the runoff from fertilizers and cattle waste. The activities of a growing human population contribute greatly to water pollution, as well.

EVERGLADES FOREVER ACT

The Everglades Forever Act was passed to reduce the high levels of phosphorus and other pollutants being dumped into the Everglades. The 1994 legislation places on farmers the responsibility for paying to clean up the water that leaves their farms. In addition, 40,000

Phosphorus and Farming

Sawgrass does not grow well in water that has a lot of phosphorus. In the 1980s it was discovered that Everglades sawgrass was dying and being replaced by cattails, which thrive in a high-phosphorus environment. This indicated that the phosphorus level in the Everglades was rising. Moreover, plants and animals that relied on the diminishing supply of sawgrass were being harmed.

In 1962 the U.S. government established an agricultural area on 1,181 square miles (3,059 sq km) of land south of Lake Okeechobee and north of Everglades National Park. Relations between the United States and the new Cuban government of Fidel Castro had grown hostile, and policy makers in Washington wanted to end U.S. reliance on sugar imported from Cuba. For this reason, growers were encouraged to plant sugarcane in the Everglades Agricultural Area. Several big sugar concerns and some vegetable growers soon began to farm the area, and they used the customary phosphorus-based fertilizers.

When high phosphorus levels were discovered in the Everglades and attributed to fertilizers, a legal battle began and continued for many years. The sugar industry stated that phosphorus was good for plants and was harmless if not present in excess. But after many tests, scientists discovered that extremely low levels of phosphorus had made the natural Everglades unique. Thus, the phosphorus added by agricultural efforts had in fact imperiled the chemical balance in the Glades. Even so, state and local government officials were slow to take action. After all, the federal government had asked farmers to use the Everglades Agricultural Area in the first place. Eventually, in 1994, the Everglades Forever Act was passed to address the phosphorus problem.

acres (16,190 ha) was set aside to make filtering marshes to treat water from farms and cities. Farm water runoff would also be tested. Because of the Everglades Forever Act, water coming from farms had reduced phosphorus levels by 73 percent.

THE COMPREHENSIVE EVERGLADES RESTORATION PLAN

South Florida's water supply is being destroyed. Now joining environmentalists in their concerns are farmers, bankers, and developers.

It was obvious that the original system of canals and levees was no longer useful. This system was funneling about 1.7 billion gallons (6.4 billion liters) of freshwater into the Atlantic Ocean and the Gulf of Mexico. Wasting that much water in South Florida today is unthinkable.

Under the circumstances, the Army Corps of Engineers was asked to work out a plan to fix the water problems they had created in South Florida decades ago. Working around the clock, the engineers put together a restudy team consisting of biologists, engineers, and **hydrologists**. In 1999 the group submitted to Congress a $10.5 billion plan to change the canal and water distribution system in South Florida. This scheme, which would be the most expensive environmental restoration ever, would not come to completion for about thirty years. On December 11, 2000, President Clinton signed a bill to execute the plan. Once approved, this plan took on the name of Comprehensive Everglades Restoration Plan, or CERP. Its purpose is to restore the water flow in the Everglades to as close to a natural state as possible.

Throughout the years, the water flow to the Everglades had been reduced from over 450 billion gallons (1.7 trillion liters) to 260 billion gallons (985 billion liters). This shortage of water has severely affected the animal and plant life of the Everglades. One restoration project, scheduled for completion in 2010, aims to increase the flow of water to the Everglades to around 325 billion gallons (1.3 trillion liters). Because that much additional water could flood the Tamiami Trail, two bridges have been planned. These bridges would lift the road in one section for 2 miles (3.2 km) and in another section for 1 mile (1.6 km). These open areas would allow the water to flow as a slow-moving river, similar to its natural state.

In 2006 more than 30 million tons of earth was moved to make way for a 16,700-acre reservoir, which will restore the natural flow of water to the Everglades.

Another important step in this plan is to remove all levees and canals in the section of land north of the Tamiami Trail east of Big Cypress National Preserve. Reservoirs above and below ground would be established, as well as aquifers. Pumps fitted into the aquifers would allow the dispersal of water into areas that have low water levels. More filter marshes would be created to improve water quality.

The goal would be to restore the natural ebb and flow of water into the Everglades. The plants and animals of the Everglades would then be provided with the amount of water they need to survive. This would help wading birds, fish, frogs, and alligators to flourish. In addition, Florida residents would have the water they need.

THE DISAPPEARING FLORIDA PANTHER

There are more plants and animals that face extinction in the Everglades than in any other U.S. national park. One of the most endangered animals is the Florida panther. Hundreds of years ago, these big cats could be found not only in Florida but also in other southeastern states such as Mississippi, Louisiana, Alabama, and Georgia. Other endangered species include the American crocodile, the hawksbill turtle, and the wood stork.

Several factors have contributed to the shrinking of the Florida panther population. First, their habitat is being taken away. Adult male Florida panthers need roaming areas up to 200 square miles (520 sq km). Today, they are found in a small area in southern Florida near the Big Cypress National Preserve and Everglades National Park. There have been reported sightings of the Florida panther in Arkansas, Florida, and Louisiana, but none have been confirmed.

Florida Panthers are losing their natural habitat as the land area of the Everglades diminishes.

The Florida panther is also threatened by traffic. Its small habitat is surrounded by four-lane freeways, constructed to support the population boom in South Florida. In the past, many Florida panthers were killed by motorists. To decrease the number of such accidents, wildlife crossings have been built under a major freeway, as well as tall fences to funnel the panthers into the crossings instead of taking their chances on the road.

Another problem affecting the Florida panther's survival is **inbreeding**. Today there are only a few dozen Florida panthers.

Because of these low numbers, opportunities to mate with animals from different families are greatly diminished, and birth defects are common. For example, some male panther kittens have been born with deformities that prevent them from siring offspring. The U.S. Fish and Wildlife Service came up with an idea to combat the inbreeding problem. They began bringing in Texas cougars, one of the Florida panther's closest relatives. Breeding the Florida panther with the Texas cougar has produced healthy kittens.

SAVING THE MANATEES

Another endangered animal in the Everglades is the West Indian manatee. These mammals are among the gentlest creatures alive, especially given their size. The heavy, slow-moving manatees are having a hard time surviving, mostly because of speeding boaters, who do not give the sea creature time to swim out of the way. Often the manatees' thick hides

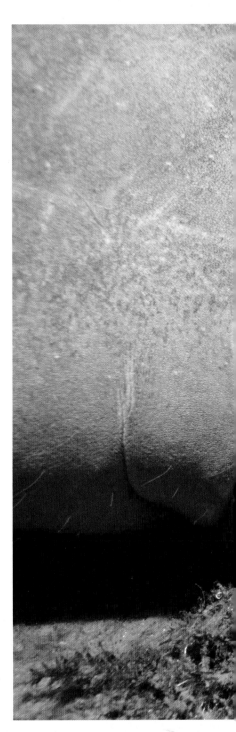

Manatees are under threat due to the ❧ *sharp blades of motorboats that course their way through their natural habit.*

are sliced open by propellers, causing fatal wounds. Injuries from propellers are so common that scientists now identify individual manatees by the "prop scars" on their tails or backs.

Boaters are also destroying sea grass, the manatees' main food. Especially in Florida Bay, where the water is sometimes only 3 to 4 feet (0.9 m to 1.2 m) deep, speedboat motors are scarring sea grass beds. Recovery can take ten to twenty years.

To protect manatees from speeding boats, no-wake zones have been established. Public education has also begun with the goal of teaching boaters how to safely steer through the shallow waters and explaining to them how much damage careless boating practices cause.

Invasive Species

Plants and animals that are not originally from the Everglades are harming the ecosystems of this unique region. Invasive species such as Brazilian peppers and Australian pines have been found in many sections of the Everglades. In addition, reptiles such as the Burmese python and the Nile monitor lizard have made the Everglades their home. Millions of dollars have been budgeted toward ridding Everglades National Park of invasive species and reintroducing native plants and animals into the park.

GLOBAL WARMING AND THE EVERGLADES

There is no doubt that the amount of carbon dioxide in the atmosphere has increased. Scientists have also proven that air and sea temperatures are rising. The rise in the global sea level predicted by some, 7 inches (18 cm) to about 2 feet (60 cm) within the next ninety-five years, could affect the Everglades dramatically, as the majority of the park is at elevations lower than 3 feet (90 cm).

If the sea level rises rapidly, entire mangrove forests could be destroyed. In addition, freshwater habitats could be washed out by seawater. The managers and scientists who oversee Everglades National Park are very aware of these possibilities. They have been taking several actions to minimize the damage of future global warming. One action is to restore the park as much as possible to its natural state. This is being done by CERP. The idea is that a restored Everglades would be better able to withstand global changes.

Another change affects the construction of park facilities. Visitor centers could be built on stilts. Another idea is to bring mobile buildings in for park facilities. When a storm or surge is predicted, the buildings could be moved further inland. Also, all fixed docks could be replaced with floating docks that adjust to sea levels.

THE FUTURE OF THE EVERGLADES

Humans have destroyed the natural water flow of the Everglades. It is up to us to fix this problem. Scientists and engineers currently

Through restoration projects, the Everglades will hopefully remain a vital natural habitat for all living species that make it their home.

working on the huge Everglades restoration plan are excited and hopeful. Citizens can also help by joining organizations dedicated to saving the Everglades. If all the plans for the Everglades are completed, the majority of the beautiful natural area called Everglades National Park will be restored. This will ensure that the Everglades will be here for many generations to come.

Glossary

aquifers   underground layers of rock that hold water

basin   an area of land drained by a river and its branches

brackish water   a mix of freshwater and salt water

ceded   surrendered or gave up one's right to something

clan   several families who are descended from the same ancestor

ecosystem   all the plants and animals that live in a certain environment

environmentalist   a person who works to protect the natural environment

estivate   to pass time in a state of no motion, as if asleep

hydrologists   scientists who study the effects and distribution of water

inbreeding   mating or producing of offspring by parents that are closely related

levees   banks built next to a river to keep it from overflowing

lichen   a combination of a fungus and an alga

peat   decaying plant life formed in marshes

phosphorus   a chemical element used in producing fertilizers, cleaners, and fine china

plumes   large, fluffy feathers

sedge   a stiff grass that grows in water

sloughs   depressions or shallow cracks in land that are usually covered by slow-moving water

stands   groups of growing trees

U.S. Army Corps of Engineers   the scientists and engineers who are responsible for maintaining and developing the nation's water supply

Fast Facts

Official name: Everglades National Park

Date of discovery: First Europeans visited the area early in the sixteenth century

Date dedicated: December 6, 1947

Location: Southernmost tip of Florida

Total land area: 1,509,000 acres (610,670 ha)

Highest natural elevation: 8 feet (2.4 m)

Lowest elevation: Sea level

Average temperature: Wet season 90°F (32°C), dry season 77°F (25°C)

Average yearly precipitation: 60 inches (152 cm)

Population: Park staff personnel, about 80 to 150 people; Miccosukee (not all living within the boundaries of Everglades National Park), about 550 people

Famous areas: Ten Thousand Islands, Royal Palm, Florida Bay

Famous visitors: President Harry S. Truman, President George H. W. Bush

Plants: Slash pine, gumbo limbo tree, ghost orchid, butterfly orchid, sawgrass

Animals: West Indian manatee, Florida panther, great blue heron, roseate spoonbill, snowy white egret, bald eagle, Everglades kite

Greatest threats: Surrounding population, which is affecting water supply and water quality

Everglades kite

Find Out More

BOOKS

Hart, Joyce. *Florida*. New York: Marshall Cavendish Benchmark, 2007.

King, David C. *The Seminole*. New York: Marshall Cavendish Benchmark, 2007.

Lynch, Wayne. *The Everglades, Our Wild World*. Minnetonka, MN: Northword Press, 2007.

DVDs

Everglades: Florida's River of Grass, Pro-Active Entertainment, 2007.

Water's Journey—Everglades: Currents of Change, Karst Productions, 2006.

The Best of: Everglades National Park, International Video Projects, 2004.

WEB SITES

Everglades National Park

www.nps.gov/ever/

Visit this site for information about visiting Everglades National Park and the history, culture, nature, and science of the park.

Friends of the Everglades

www.everglades.org

For the latest local news on saving the Everglades and for learning how to become a friend of the Everglades see this site.

Save the Manatee Club

www.savethemanatee.org/

This site provides information on how to adopt a manatee, manatee habits, and manatee news.

Index

Page numbers in **boldface** are illustrations and charts.

ABOUT THE AUTHOR

Sara Louise Kras is the author of more than nineteen books for children, including *The Galapagos Islands* and *Antigua and Barbuda* for Marshall Cavendish Benchmark. She grew up in Washington State, Texas, and Colorado. A lifelong lover of the outdoors, she lives in Glendale, California, with her husband, daughter, and cat.

While visiting the Everglades, Kras enjoyed listening to the wind blow across the vast sawgrass prairie at Pa-hay-okee Overlook. On the shore of Pine Glades Lake, she stood still while an alligator swam over to get a closer look. Looking down from an observation tower at Shark Valley, she spotted a huge snapping turtle swimming in the deep Shark Valley Slough. Kras says, "I have always been fascinated with the world. Seeing people, landscapes, and animals different from where I live is so exciting! Finding out about all the world's treasures and beautiful places and then telling children about them is one of my favorite things to do. I love to get children excited about the world they live in and to get them curious to find out more."